# *MASTERING BUSINESS CREDIT*

## *A Comprehensive Guide to Building and Managing Your Business Credit*

### BY

### CANDICE & JOSHUA HARRIS

# Table of Contents

# CHAPTER 1:

## Introduction

### The Importance of Business Credit

In the world of business, credit isn't just a personal financial concern; it's a vital component of your company's financial health. Business credit is the lifeline that can enable your venture to thrive, grow, and succeed. This chapter will lay the groundwork for your journey to mastering business credit by highlighting its importance and the benefits it can bring to your enterprise.

### Why Business Credit Matters

Business credit is a measure of your company's financial responsibility and creditworthiness in the eyes of creditors, lenders, suppliers, and potential partners. Just as your personal credit score impacts your ability to secure loans or favorable interest rates, your business credit profile plays a pivotal role in your company's financial future. Here's why it matters:

1. **Access to Capital**: A strong business credit profile can open doors to funding opportunities, such as loans, lines of credit, and business credit cards. These financial resources can be crucial for launching new products, expanding operations, or weathering unexpected financial challenges.

2. **Supplier Relationships**: Suppliers often extend credit terms to businesses with good credit, allowing you to negotiate better payment terms. This can improve your cash flow and help you manage your finances more effectively.

3. **Growth and Expansion**: Building business credit can enable you to pursue growth and expansion opportunities that would otherwise be out of reach. Whether it's opening new locations, investing in equipment, or hiring additional staff, credit can be a catalyst for growth.

4. **Credibility**: A strong credit profile can enhance your company's credibility in the eyes of customers, partners, and investors. It signals that your business is financially responsible and stable, fostering trust and confidence.

5. **Risk Management**: Business credit can help you manage financial risk. By maintaining a solid credit profile, you're better prepared to navigate economic downturns or unexpected challenges

without relying solely on your personal finances.

## Benefits of Establishing Strong Business Credit

As you embark on the journey to build and manage your business credit, it's essential to understand the tangible benefits it can bring to your company:

1. **Lower Interest Rates**: With strong credit, you're more likely to qualify for loans and credit cards with lower interest rates. This can save your business significant money in interest payments over time.

2. **Higher Credit Limits**: A robust credit history can lead to higher credit limits on business credit cards and lines of credit,

providing you with greater financial flexibility.

3. **Favorable Payment Terms**: Suppliers may offer you more extended payment terms, allowing you to pay for goods and services over an extended period, improving your cash flow.

4. **Business Growth**: As mentioned earlier, good credit can be a catalyst for business growth, enabling you to seize opportunities and invest in your company's future.

5. **Competitive Advantage**: Having strong business credit can give you a competitive advantage when bidding for contracts or seeking partnerships. It demonstrates your financial stability and commitment to responsible business practices.

6. **Separation of Personal and Business Finances**: Building business credit allows you to separate your personal and business finances further, reducing personal liability and simplifying tax reporting.

In the chapters that follow, you'll learn how to lay the foundation for strong business credit, establish a business credit profile, and manage your credit responsibly. With the right knowledge and strategies, you can harness the power of business credit to propel your company toward long-term success.

# CHAPTER 2
## Understanding Business Credit

### What is Business Credit?

Business credit refers to a company's creditworthiness and financial reputation in the eyes of creditors, lenders, suppliers, and other business partners. It's an essential aspect of any successful venture and plays a crucial role in determining your ability to access financing, secure favorable terms with suppliers, and establish credibility in the business world.

### Differentiating Personal and Business Credit

While personal and business credit share similarities, they are distinct entities. Understanding these differences is essential for managing your business credit effectively:

- **Ownership and Liability**: Personal credit is tied to an individual's financial history and is used to assess personal loans, mortgages, and credit cards. In contrast, business credit evaluates the financial health of a company and helps determine its ability to repay business-related debts. Establishing business credit allows you to separate personal and business finances, reducing personal liability.

- **Credit Reporting Agencies**: Personal credit is typically reported by consumer credit bureaus like Equifax, Experian, and TransUnion. Business credit, on the other hand, is reported by business credit bureaus such as Dun & Bradstreet, Experian Business, and Equifax Business.

- **Factors Affecting Credit Scores**:
Personal credit scores are influenced by
factors like personal credit history, debt-
to-income ratio, and payment history on
personal debts. Business credit scores
consider factors such as payment history
with business creditors, trade references,
public records, and financial data.

## How Business Credit Scores are Calculated

Understanding how business credit scores
are determined is crucial for proactively
managing your business's
creditworthiness. Here are some key
factors that influence business credit
scores:

1. **Payment History** This is one of the
most critical aspects of your business

credit score. It reflects your track record of making payments on time. Consistently paying bills promptly demonstrates financial responsibility.

2. **Credit Utilization**: Similar to personal credit, business credit scores consider the ratio of your outstanding debt to your available credit. Maintaining a low credit utilization rate indicates responsible use of credit.

3. **Length of Credit History**: Just as with personal credit, the length of time you've had active credit accounts can positively impact your business credit score. It demonstrates a track record of financial responsibility.

4. **Public Records**: Negative information like bankruptcies, liens, or judgments can significantly impact your business credit

score. Avoiding these issues is crucial for maintaining a healthy credit profile.

5. **Industry Risk**: Some business credit bureaus take into account the risk associated with specific industries. For example, industries with higher rates of business failures may have slightly different scoring criteria.

6. **Size and Financial Stability of Your Business**: The size and financial stability of your business, as well as industry benchmarks, can influence your credit score. A larger, more established business may be viewed more favorably.

7. **Trade References**: Positive feedback from suppliers and vendors can boost your business credit score. Establishing good relationships with these partners can have a positive impact.

In the following chapters, we'll delve deeper into strategies for optimizing these factors and building a strong business credit profile. By understanding the nuances of business credit and proactively managing it, you'll be better positioned to leverage credit for the benefit of your business.

# CHAPTER 3

## Setting Up Your Business for Credit Success

### Choosing the Right Business Structure

Selecting the appropriate legal structure for your business is a critical step in establishing a strong foundation for business credit. The structure you choose will affect how your business is taxed, how profits and losses are distributed, and the extent of your personal liability. Here are some common business structures and their implications for credit:

1. **Sole Proprietorship**:
   - **Ownership**: Owned and operated by a single individual.
   - **Liability**: The owner is personally liable for business debts and obligations.

- **Credit Implications**: Business and personal finances are typically considered one entity. Establishing business credit can be more challenging, but personal credit may play a significant role.

2. **Partnership**:
   - **Ownership**: Shared by two or more individuals who manage the business together.
   - **Liability**: Partners are personally liable for business debts and obligations.
   - **Credit Implications**: Similar to a sole proprietorship, business and personal finances are closely linked. It may be necessary to rely on personal credit initially.

3. **Limited Liability Company (LLC):**
   - **Ownership**: Combines elements of a partnership and a corporation, providing limited liability to owners (members).

- **Liability:** Members' personal assets are typically protected from business debts.
- **Credit Implications**: An LLC's credit profile is separate from its members. It's important to establish and build business credit independently.

## 4. **Corporation**:
- **Ownership**: A legal entity separate from its owners (shareholders).
- **Liability**: Shareholders' personal assets are generally shielded from business debts.
- **Credit Implications**: Corporations have their own credit profiles, distinct from those of their shareholders. Building business credit is crucial.

## 5. **S Corporation**:
- **Ownership**: A type of corporation that elects to pass business income, deductions, and credits through to its shareholders for federal tax purposes.

- **Liability**: Shareholders have limited personal liability for business debts.
- **Credit Implications**: Similar to a standard corporation, it's essential to establish and build business credit.

## Registering Your Business

Once you've determined the appropriate legal structure, you'll need to register your business with the appropriate government authorities. This process may vary depending on your location and business structure. Common steps include:

- **Choose a Business Name**: Ensure it's unique and adheres to any naming conventions in your jurisdiction.

- **Register with the State**: File the necessary paperwork with your state's business registration office. This may include articles of incorporation (for corporations), articles of organization (for LLCs), or other registration forms.

- **Obtain Necessary Permits and Licenses**: Depending on your industry and location, you may need specific permits or licenses to operate legally.

**Obtaining an EIN** (Employer Identification Number)

An EIN is a unique identifier assigned by the Internal Revenue Service (IRS) to businesses for tax purposes. It's like a social security number for your business. You'll need an EIN to open a business bank account, apply for business licenses, and establish credit accounts in your business's name.

You can apply for an EIN online through the IRS website or by submitting Form SS-4.

By taking these steps to set up your business properly, you'll lay a solid foundation for building and managing your business credit. In the subsequent chapters, we'll delve into the practical strategies for establishing a robust business credit profile.

# CHAPTER 4
## Building a Solid Foundation

### Opening Business Bank Accounts

One of the fundamental steps in establishing a solid foundation for your business credit is opening dedicated business bank accounts. This separation of personal and business finances is crucial for building a distinct financial identity for your company.

### Benefits of Business Bank Accounts:

1. **Legal Protection**: Maintaining separate accounts helps protect your personal assets in case of legal issues or financial liabilities related to your business.

2. **Simplified Bookkeeping**: Having separate accounts makes it easier to track and manage business expenses, revenue, and financial transactions.

3. **Professionalism**: It demonstrates a level of professionalism to clients, suppliers, and partners, reinforcing the legitimacy of your business.

4. **Easier Financial Reporting**: Separate accounts facilitate accurate financial reporting and tax filing, which can be critical for obtaining business credit.

5. **Facilitates Credit Applications**: Many lenders and creditors require proof of a dedicated business bank account when considering credit applications.

**Establishing a Business Phone Line**

A separate business phone line further emphasizes the distinction between your personal affairs and your business operations. It's a professional touch that can instill confidence in clients and partners.

**Options for Business Phone Lines:**

1. **Landline:** Traditional phone lines are reliable and familiar to many clients. Consider a local or toll-free number.

2. **Virtual Phone System**: Internet-based phone systems offer flexibility and a range of features, including call forwarding, voicemail, and professional greetings.

3. **Mobile Business Line**: A dedicated mobile number for business calls can be convenient, especially for entrepreneurs on the go.

## Setting Up a Professional Business Address

Having a physical business address, separate from your home address, adds credibility to your enterprise. It provides a stable point of contact for clients, suppliers, and creditors.

**Options for Business Addresses:**

1. **Commercial Office Space**: Renting office space is a traditional option, offering a professional environment and a central location.

2. **Virtual Office Services**: These services provide a physical address and may include mail handling and occasional use of meeting spaces.

3. **Co-Working Spaces**: Shared workspaces offer a professional environment without the long-term commitment of leasing an office.

4. **Mailbox Rental Services**: Many postal and shipping centers offer mailbox rental services with a street address, providing a professional appearance.

By establishing dedicated business accounts, a professional phone line, and a distinct business address, you're creating a clear separation between your personal and business affairs. This separation is not only beneficial for day-to-day operations but also lays the groundwork for a strong business credit profile. In the following chapters, we'll dive deeper into strategies for building and managing business credit effectively.

# CHAPTER 5
## Creating a Business Credit Profile

Creating a robust business credit profile is essential for accessing credit, securing favorable terms, and demonstrating your company's financial responsibility. In this chapter, we'll explore the steps involved in building your business credit profile.

### Vendor Credit Accounts

Vendor credit accounts are one of the primary tools for building business credit. These are accounts established with suppliers who provide goods or services to your business on credit. Here's how to get started:

1. **Select Reliable Suppliers**: Choose reputable suppliers who report payment

history to business credit bureaus. They could be office supply companies, equipment providers, or industry-specific suppliers.

2. **Apply for Credit**: Contact your chosen suppliers and inquire about opening a credit account. They may request information about your business, such as your EIN, financial statements, and references.

3. **Use Credit Responsibly**: Once approved, make regular purchases and ensure timely payments. Paying invoices on time or ahead of schedule is crucial for building a positive payment history.

4. **Verify Reporting**: Check with your suppliers to confirm that they report your payment history to business credit bureaus. Not all vendors report, so it's essential to

ensure that your responsible credit use is being documented.

### Business Credit Cards

Business credit cards are versatile financial tools that can help establish and build your business credit profile:

1. **Choose the Right Card**: Select a business credit card with features that align with your business needs. Look for cards that report to business credit bureaus.

2. **Apply Responsibly**: When applying, provide accurate business information, and be prepared for a credit check. Approval may be based on both your business and personal credit.

3. **Use Wisely**: Use the card for business expenses and maintain low credit

utilization (ideally below 30% of the credit limit). Pay the balance in full each month to avoid interest charges.

4. **Monitor and Manage**: Regularly review your card statements, track expenses, and ensure timely payments. Consistent, on-time payments contribute positively to your business credit profile.

## Trade Lines and Net Terms

Trade lines refer to credit arrangements with suppliers or creditors that extend payment terms. For example, if a supplier offers "Net-30" terms, you have 30 days to pay the invoice. Building trade lines can enhance your credit profile:

1. **Negotiate Terms**: When establishing relationships with suppliers, negotiate

favorable payment terms, such as Net-30, Net-60, or Net-90.

2. **Timely Payments:** Always meet payment deadlines to demonstrate financial responsibility.

3. **Increase Credit Limits**: Over time, you can request higher credit limits on trade lines as your business credit profile strengthens.

4. **Diverse Trade Lines**: Building relationships with multiple suppliers and creditors diversifies your trade lines and further enhances your business credit.

By actively managing vendor credit accounts, using business credit cards responsibly, and establishing trade lines with favorable payment terms, you'll lay a solid foundation for your business credit profile. In the following chapters, we'll delve into more advanced strategies for managing and optimizing your business credit.

# CHAPTER 6

## Managing Business Credit Responsibly

Managing your business credit responsibly is essential for maintaining a strong credit profile and ensuring access to favorable credit terms. In this chapter, we'll explore key principles and strategies for responsible credit management.

### Paying Bills on Time

Timely payments are the cornerstone of a strong business credit profile. Consistently paying your bills by their due dates demonstrates financial responsibility and reliability to creditors and suppliers. Here are some tips:

- **Set Reminders**: Use calendars, reminders, or accounting software to track payment due dates.
- **Automate Payments**: Consider setting up automatic payments for recurring bills to ensure they're paid on time.
- **Establish Cash Flow Management**: Maintain a healthy cash flow to ensure you have the funds available to cover expenses when they come due.

### Avoiding High Credit Utilization

Credit utilization refers to the percentage of your available credit that you're using at any given time. High utilization can negatively impact your credit score. To manage this:

- **Monitor Utilization Rates**: Regularly review your credit card balances and credit

limits to ensure you're not using too high a percentage of your available credit.
- **Pay Down Balances**: If you're approaching high utilization, make efforts to pay down balances to reduce the percentage of credit being used.

## Monitoring Your Business Credit Report

Regularly monitoring your business credit report allows you to spot errors, identify areas for improvement, and address any negative information promptly. Here's how to do it:

- **Obtain and Review Your Report**: Request your business credit report from major business credit bureaus like Dun & Bradstreet, Experian Business, and Equifax Business. Review it for accuracy and completeness.

- **Dispute Errors**: If you identify inaccuracies or errors, dispute them with the respective credit bureau. Provide supporting documentation to rectify the issue.
- **Stay Informed**: Subscribe to credit monitoring services or set up alerts to receive notifications of changes to your business credit profile.

## Managing Debt Responsibly

While credit can be a valuable tool for business growth, it's crucial to use it judiciously. Here are some guidelines for responsible debt management:

- **Borrow Wisely**: Only take on debt when it's necessary and when you have a clear plan for how it will contribute to your business's growth or profitability.

- **Budget for Debt Repayment**: Ensure that your budget includes provisions for repaying any debt you take on, including interest and fees.
- **Diversify Your Credit Portfolio:** Avoid over-reliance on one type of credit. Having a mix of credit accounts, such as loans, credit cards, and trade lines, can demonstrate diverse credit management.

By following these principles of responsible credit management, you'll not only maintain a strong business credit profile but also position your business for long-term financial success. In the upcoming chapters, we'll explore more advanced strategies for leveraging business credit to support your business's growth and expansion.

# CHAPTER 7
## Building Relationships with Suppliers and Lenders

Establishing strong relationships with suppliers and lenders is crucial for your business's financial health and growth. In this chapter, we'll delve into practical strategies for cultivating these important connections.

### Cultivating Strong Vendor Relationships

Maintaining positive relationships with your suppliers goes beyond transactional interactions. It can lead to more favorable terms, increased trust, and even potential referrals. Here's how to nurture these relationships:

1. **Communication**: Keep lines of communication open. Understand their business needs and share yours. Regularly update them on changes within your company.

2. **Timely Payments**: Consistently pay your invoices on time or ahead of schedule. This demonstrates reliability and fosters trust.

3. **Negotiate Win-Win Terms**: Seek mutually beneficial terms. For example, you might negotiate longer payment terms in exchange for larger or more frequent orders.

4. **Provide Feedback**: Offer constructive feedback on their products or services. This can strengthen your partnership and lead to improvements that benefit both parties.

**Building Credit with Suppliers**

Strong supplier relationships can also play
a vital role in building your business credit
profile:

1. **Choose Suppliers Who Report**:
Prioritize suppliers who report your
payment history to business credit bureaus.
This can positively impact your credit
profile.

2. **Request Credit References**: Ask your
suppliers for credit references. These
references can vouch for your business's
creditworthiness when seeking credit from
other sources.

3. **Gradually Increase Orders**: As your
business credit profile strengthens,
consider gradually increasing your order

volumes with trusted suppliers. This can
lead to larger credit limits.

**Approaching Lenders for Business
Loans**

Lenders can be valuable partners in
funding your business's growth. Here are
steps to take when seeking business loans:

1. **Prepare a Strong Loan Application**:
Provide comprehensive financial
statements, a well-articulated business
plan, and any other documents required by
the lender.

2. **Research Lenders**: Identify lenders that
specialize in your industry or offer the type
of financing you need. Different lenders
may have varying criteria and terms.

3. **Build Your Business Credit Profile**: A strong credit profile is essential when applying for loans. Demonstrating responsible credit management boosts your credibility.

4. **Establish Relationships Before You Need Funding**: Building relationships with lenders before you require financing can make the application process smoother.

5. **Understand the Terms**: Carefully review the terms and conditions of any loan offer. Pay attention to interest rates, repayment schedules, and any collateral requirements.

Remember, building relationships with suppliers and lenders is a two-way street. It's not just about what they can do for you, but also about how you can contribute to their success. By cultivating strong, mutually beneficial partnerships, you'll have a network of support that can help propel your business forward. In the following chapters, we'll explore additional strategies for leveraging business credit to drive growth and expansion.

# CHAPTER 8
## Securing Business Credit Cards and Lines of Credit

Business credit cards and lines of credit are powerful financial tools that can provide flexibility and support your business's financial needs. In this chapter, we'll explore how to effectively utilize these resources.

### Choosing the Right Business Credit Card

Selecting the right business credit card is crucial for optimizing your financial management. Consider the following factors when making your choice:

1. **Interest Rates**: Look for cards with competitive interest rates, especially if you

anticipate carrying a balance from month to month.

2. **Rewards and Benefits**: Some cards offer rewards like cash back, travel points, or discounts on specific business expenses. Choose a card with rewards that align with your business needs.

3. **Annual Fees**: Consider whether the benefits of the card justify any annual fees. Some cards offer substantial rewards or perks that outweigh the cost.

4. **Credit Limit**: Ensure the card's credit limit aligns with your business's financial needs. A higher limit provides greater flexibility but also requires responsible management.

5. **Reporting to Business Credit Bureaus**: Verify that the card issuer

reports your payment history to business credit bureaus. This is crucial for building your business credit profile.

**Using Business Credit Cards Wisely**

Once you've acquired a business credit card, it's important to use it responsibly. Here are some best practices:

1. **Separate Business and Personal Expenses**: Use the card exclusively for business expenses to maintain clear financial records.

2. **Pay in Full Each Month**: Paying the full balance each month helps avoid interest charges and demonstrates financial responsibility to creditors.

3. **Track Expenses**: Keep detailed records of all expenses made with the card. This

helps with budgeting, accounting, and tax reporting.

4. **Monitor Statements**: Regularly review your card statements for accuracy and report any discrepancies promptly.

## Maximizing Rewards and Benefits

Many business credit cards offer additional benefits beyond credit. Make sure you're taking full advantage of these perks:

1. **Cash Back or Rewards Programs**: Understand how you can earn and redeem cash back or rewards points. Some cards offer bonus categories for increased rewards.

2. **Travel Benefits**: If your card offers travel perks, such as airline miles or

lounge access, familiarize yourself with how to utilize them for maximum value.

3. **Insurance Coverage**: Some business credit cards offer travel insurance, rental car insurance, or purchase protection. Understand the coverage provided.

4. **Business Tools and Resources**: Some cards offer access to business management tools, expense tracking, and financial reporting features.

By selecting the right business credit card, using it responsibly, and maximizing the benefits it offers, you can leverage this financial tool to support your business's growth and success. In the subsequent chapters, we'll explore additional strategies for optimizing your business credit profile.

# CHAPTER 9
## Establishing Business Lines of Credit

Business lines of credit provide a valuable source of flexible financing that can be crucial for managing cash flow, seizing opportunities, and covering unexpected expenses. In this chapter, we'll delve into how to establish and effectively use business lines of credit.

## Understanding Business Lines of Credit

A business line of credit is a revolving credit facility that allows you to borrow up to a predetermined limit. Unlike a term loan, where you receive a lump sum and make fixed payments, a line of credit provides ongoing access to funds, which you can draw on as needed.

**Advantages of a Business Line of Credit:**

1. **Flexibility**: You can borrow and repay funds as needed, up to your approved limit.

2. **Interest Only on Utilized Amount**: You're only charged interest on the portion of the credit line you use.

3. **Quick Access to Funds**: Once established, you can access funds quickly, which can be crucial for seizing time-sensitive opportunities.

4. **Cash Flow Management**: It provides a safety net for managing cash flow gaps, especially in seasonal or cyclical industries.

**Qualifying for a Business Line of Credit**

Lenders evaluate several factors when considering your eligibility for a business line of credit:

1. **Creditworthiness**: Both your personal and business credit scores will be considered. A strong credit history demonstrates your ability to manage credit responsibly.

2. **Business Financials**: Lenders may review your business's financial statements, including revenue, expenses, and profitability.

3. **Time in Business**: Some lenders require a minimum period of operation before considering your application. This can vary depending on the lender.

4. **Collateral (if required)**: Depending on the lender and the size of the credit line, they may require collateral to secure the credit facility.

5. **Business Plan and Purpose**: Some lenders may ask for a business plan outlining how you intend to use the line of credit and how it will benefit your business.

## Using Business Lines of Credit Effectively

Once you have a business line of credit in place, it's important to manage it wisely:

1. **Have a Clear Purpose**: Use the line of credit for specific, well-defined purposes, such as inventory purchase, equipment acquisition, or covering short-term operational expenses.

**2. Monitor Your Credit Utilization:**
Avoid maxing out your credit line.
Keeping your utilization below 30% is
generally advisable.

**3. Make Timely Payments**: Pay back any
borrowed funds promptly. This not only
reduces interest costs but also
demonstrates financial responsibility to
lenders.

**4. Revisit and Adjust Limits:** As your
business grows, you may need to request
an increase in your credit limit to
accommodate larger financial needs.

By understanding how business lines of
credit work, qualifying for one, and using
it strategically, you can leverage this
financial tool to support your business's
financial stability and growth. In the

following chapters, we'll explore more advanced strategies for optimizing your business credit profile.

# CHAPTER 10

## Applying for Small Business Loans

Small business loans are a critical source of capital for many enterprises. Whether you're looking to expand operations, launch new products, or cover unexpected expenses, understanding the loan application process is essential. In this chapter, we'll explore how to navigate the process effectively.

### Types of Small Business Loans

Before applying for a small business loan, it's important to understand the different types of loans available. Each type serves specific purposes and may have different application requirements:

1. **Term Loans**: These are traditional loans where you receive a lump sum of money upfront, which you repay over a fixed term with interest.

2. **SBA (Small Business Administration) Loans**: These government-backed loans offer favorable terms and are designed to support small businesses. They include programs like the 7(a) Loan Program and the CDC/504 Loan Program.

3. **Business Lines of Credit**: As discussed in the previous chapter, lines of credit provide flexible access to funds that you can draw on as needed.

4. **Equipment Financing**: This type of loan is specifically for purchasing equipment or machinery for your business. The equipment serves as collateral.

5. **Invoice Financing**: Also known as accounts receivable financing, this option allows you to borrow against outstanding invoices to improve cash flow.

**How to Prepare a Strong Loan Application**

A well-prepared loan application increases your chances of approval. Here's how to put together a strong application:

1. **Business Plan**: Provide a comprehensive business plan that outlines your business goals, operations, market analysis, and financial projections. This demonstrates that you have a clear strategy for using the loan.

2. **Financial Statements**: Include up-to-date financial statements, such as income statements, balance sheets, and cash flow

statements. These provide a snapshot of your business's financial health.

3. **Credit History**: Be prepared to provide both your personal and business credit history. Lenders use this information to assess your creditworthiness.

4. **Collateral (if required):** If the loan requires collateral, be prepared to detail the assets you're willing to use as security.

5. **Legal Documentation**: Depending on the lender and the type of loan, you may need to provide legal documents such as business licenses, articles of incorporation, and contracts.

6. **Repayment Plan**: Outline how you intend to repay the loan. This could include cash flow projections, revenue

forecasts, or a breakdown of how the funds
will be used.

**Navigating the Loan Approval Process**

Once you've submitted your application,
it's important to be prepared for the
approval process:

1. **Be Responsive**: Respond promptly to
any requests for additional information or
documentation from the lender.

2. **Negotiate Terms (if possible):** If you
receive a loan offer, carefully review the
terms and, if necessary, negotiate for more
favorable terms.

3. **Read the Fine Print**: Thoroughly
review the loan agreement before
accepting. Pay attention to interest rates,

repayment schedules, and any covenants or conditions.

4. **Use Funds Wisely**: Once you receive the loan, ensure that the funds are used for their intended purpose. This helps maintain financial responsibility.

By understanding the types of small business loans available, preparing a strong loan application, and navigating the approval process, you'll be better equipped to secure the financing your business needs. In the next chapters, we'll explore additional strategies for optimizing your business credit profile.

# CHAPTER 11

## Strategies for Building and Maintaining Excellent Credit

Building and maintaining excellent business credit is an ongoing process that requires careful attention and strategic management. In this chapter, we'll explore key strategies to help you achieve and sustain a strong credit profile.

### Building a Positive Payment History

One of the most influential factors in your business credit score is your payment history. Here's how to build and maintain a positive payment record:

1. **Pay on Time, Every Time**:
Consistently make payments by their due dates. Late payments can have a

significant negative impact on your credit profile.

2. **Automate Payments**: Consider setting up automatic payments for your recurring bills and credit accounts to ensure they're paid on time.

3. **Negotiate Favorable Terms**: Communicate with your suppliers and creditors to negotiate terms that align with your cash flow cycle, making it easier to meet payment deadlines.

4. **Monitor Payment Performance**: Regularly review your credit reports to confirm that your payment history is being accurately reported.

**Managing Debt Responsibly**

Effectively managing your business's debt load is crucial for maintaining a healthy credit profile. Here are some tips:

1. **Borrow Wisely**: Only take on debt for necessary expenses or opportunities that will contribute to your business's growth or profitability.

2. **Budget for Repayment**: Ensure that your budget includes provisions for repaying any debt you take on, including interest and fees.

3. **Diversify Credit Types**: Having a mix of credit accounts, such as loans, credit cards, and trade lines, can demonstrate diverse credit management.

**Strategic Use of Credit**

Using credit strategically can help you achieve specific business goals. Consider these approaches:

1. **Seasonal Financing**: Use credit to cover expenses during slow seasons, with a plan to repay it during peak periods.

2. **Investment in Growth:** Leverage credit for initiatives that will lead to business growth, such as expanding operations, upgrading equipment, or hiring additional staff.

3. **Emergency Fund**: Maintain a line of credit or reserves for unexpected expenses or opportunities that may arise.

4. **Capitalizing on Opportunities**: Be prepared to seize time-sensitive opportunities, such as purchasing inventory at a discounted rate or taking

advantage of a limited-time business expansion opportunity.

**Monitoring and Reviewing Your Credit Profile**

Regularly monitoring your business credit profile is essential for catching errors, identifying areas for improvement, and addressing any negative information promptly. Here's how to do it effectively:

1. **Review Your Credit Reports**: Request and review your business credit reports from major credit bureaus. Check for accuracy and completeness.

2. **Dispute Inaccuracies**: If you identify inaccuracies or errors, dispute them with the respective credit bureau. Provide supporting documentation to rectify the issue.

3. **Stay Informed**: Subscribe to credit monitoring services or set up alerts to receive notifications of changes to your business credit profile.

By implementing these strategies, you'll be well-positioned to build and maintain an excellent business credit profile. This, in turn, will open up opportunities for financing and partnerships that can drive your business's success. In the upcoming chapters, we'll explore exit strategies and how they impact your business credit.

# CHAPTER 12
## Exit Strategies and Business Credit

Having a well-planned exit strategy is crucial for any business owner. It not only allows you to leave the business on your own terms but also impacts your business credit profile. In this chapter, we'll explore how different exit strategies can influence your business credit.

## Selling Your Business

Selling your business is a common exit strategy. Here's how it can affect your business credit:

1. **Transfer of Business Credit**: If the buyer agrees to assume the existing debt or credit accounts, it can help maintain your business credit profile.

2. **Closing Accounts**: If the buyer does not take over existing credit accounts, you may need to close them. This could have a temporary impact on your credit score.

3. **Debt Settlement**: If there are outstanding debts in the business's name, you may need to settle them before the sale. This can help protect your personal liability.

## Passing the Business to Family or Successors

Transitioning the business to family members or successors involves careful planning. Here's how it can affect your business credit:

1. **Transfer of Credit Accounts**: If the successors are willing and able to assume

the existing credit accounts, it can help maintain the business's credit profile.

2. **Clear Communication**: Ensure that all parties involved understand the implications for existing credit accounts and debts.

## Closing the Business

Sometimes, circumstances necessitate closing the business. Here's how it can affect your business credit:

1. **Settling Debts**: Before closing, it's essential to settle all outstanding debts and ensure that all financial obligations are met.

2. **Cancelling Accounts**: Close all credit accounts associated with the business. This

helps prevent any potential misuse of credit after closure.

**Bankruptcy**

If your business faces insurmountable financial challenges, bankruptcy might be the only option. Here's how it can affect your business credit:

1. **Negative Impact**: Bankruptcy has a significant negative impact on your business credit profile. It will be reported on your credit report and can stay for several years.

2. **Rebuilding After Bankruptcy**: After bankruptcy, focus on rebuilding your personal and business credit profiles. This will be crucial if you plan to start a new venture in the future.

**Impact on Personal Credit**

In many cases, especially for small businesses, your personal credit can be intertwined with your business's credit. Any exit strategy can have implications for your personal credit:

1. **Monitor Personal Credit**: Keep a close eye on your personal credit report, especially if your business credit is closely tied to your personal finances.

2. **Protect Personal Liability**: Take steps to protect your personal liability, especially in cases of business closure or bankruptcy.

Remember, each exit strategy has unique implications for your business credit. It's crucial to plan carefully and seek professional advice to navigate these

transitions successfully. In the final
chapters, we'll summarize key takeaways
and offer additional resources for further
guidance.

# CHAPTER 13
## Key Takeaways and Further Resources

### Key Takeaways

In this ebook, we've covered a range of topics related to building and managing business credit. Here are the key takeaways:

1. **Understanding Business Credit**: Business credit is essential for accessing financing, establishing credibility, and securing favorable terms with suppliers.

2. **Separating Personal and Business Finances**: Creating a clear division between personal and business finances is crucial for protecting personal assets and building a strong business credit profile.

3. **Setting Up Your Business for Credit Success**: Choose the right legal structure, register your business, obtain an EIN, and open dedicated business bank accounts.

4. **Establishing a Business Credit Profile**: Begin by establishing vendor credit accounts, using business credit cards responsibly, and negotiating favorable trade terms.

5. **Managing Business Credit Responsibly**: Pay bills on time, maintain a low credit utilization rate, and monitor your business credit report for accuracy.

6. **Building Relationships with Suppliers and Lenders:** Cultivate strong relationships with suppliers and lenders to enhance your business's financial stability and growth potential.

7. **Utilizing Business Credit Cards and Lines of Credit**: Choose the right credit products, use them strategically, and maximize the benefits they offer.

8. **Applying for Small Business Loans**: Understand the types of loans available, prepare a strong application, and navigate the approval process effectively.

9. **Establishing Business Lines of Credit**: Utilize business lines of credit for flexible access to funds, and manage them responsibly to maintain a healthy credit profile.

10. **Exit Strategies and Business Credit**: Plan your exit strategy carefully, considering how it will impact your business credit profile.

**Further Resources**

For more in-depth information and guidance on business credit, consider the following resources:

1. **Small Business Administration (SBA):** The SBA offers a wealth of resources and information on business credit, loans, and financial management. Visit their website at [www.sba.gov](https://www.sba.gov/).

2. **Dun & Bradstreet**: D&B provides a range of tools and resources for building and managing business credit profiles. Explore their offerings at [www.dnb.com](https://www.dnb.com/).

3. **Experian Business**: Experian offers resources, articles, and tools specifically tailored to business credit. Visit their business credit website at

[www.experian.com/business](https://ww
w.experian.com/business).

4. **Equifax Small Business**: Equifax
provides resources and tools to help
businesses understand and manage their
credit. Explore their offerings at
[www.equifax.com/business](https://www.
equifax.com/business/).

Remember, staying informed and
proactively managing your business credit
is an ongoing process. These resources can
provide valuable insights and tools to
support your efforts. Thank you for
reading this ebook, and we wish you
success in building and managing your
business credit profile!

# CHAPTER 14
## Conclusion and Final Thoughts

Congratulations on completing this ebook on building and managing business credit! We've covered a wide range of topics, from establishing a strong foundation to navigating various financial strategies.

Here are some final thoughts to keep in mind:

1. **Continuous Learning**: Business credit is a dynamic field. Stay updated on industry trends, new financial products, and changes in credit reporting practices.

2. **Financial Responsibility**: Responsible financial management is key to maintaining a strong credit profile. Pay

bills on time, manage debt wisely, and make informed financial decisions.

**3. Seek Professional Advice**: When making significant financial decisions for your business, consider seeking advice from financial advisors, accountants, or legal experts. Their expertise can be invaluable.

**4. Adaptability and Flexibility:** Businesses evolve, and so do financial needs. Be open to adjusting your strategies as your business grows and changes.

**5. Plan for the Long Term:** Building a solid business credit profile is a long-term endeavor. It requires consistent effort and vigilance.

Remember, your business credit profile is a valuable asset that can open doors to opportunities and support your business's growth. By following the principles outlined in this ebook and staying proactive in your financial management, you'll be well-equipped to navigate the world of business credit successfully.

Thank you for reading, and we wish you continued success in your business endeavors!

# Chapter 15

**Additional Resources and References**

In this final chapter, we'll provide you with a curated list of additional resources and references to further support your journey in building and managing business credit. These sources offer in-depth information, tools, and expert insights:

1. **U.S. Small Business Administration (SBA)**: The SBA provides extensive resources on business credit, loans, and financial management. Visit their website at [www.sba.gov](https://www.sba.gov/).

2. **Dun & Bradstreet (D&B):** D&B offers a range of tools and resources for building and managing business credit profiles. Explore their offerings at [www.dnb.com](https://www.dnb.com/).

3. **Experian Business**: Experian offers resources, articles, and tools tailored to business credit. Visit their business credit website at [www.experian.com/business](https://www.experian.com/business).

4. **Equifax Small Business**: Equifax provides resources and tools to help businesses understand and manage their credit. Explore their offerings at [www.equifax.com/business](https://www.equifax.com/business/).

5. **National Federation of Independent Business (NFIB)**: NFIB offers resources, advocacy, and support for small businesses. Visit their website at [www.nfib.com](https://www.nfib.com/).

6. **SCORE**: SCORE provides free mentoring and educational resources for small businesses. Find a local chapter or access their online resources at [www.score.org](https://www.score.org/).

7. **Business Credit Reports**: Obtain your business credit reports from major credit bureaus such as Dun & Bradstreet, Experian Business, and Equifax Business to monitor and manage your credit profile.

8. **Financial Advisors and Consultants**: Consider seeking advice from financial advisors, accountants, or legal experts when making significant financial decisions for your business.

9. **Industry-Specific Associations**: Depending on your business niche, consider joining industry associations that

may offer specialized resources and insights.

10. **Books on Business Credit and Financial Management**: Explore books on business credit, financial management, and entrepreneurship for in-depth knowledge on these topics.

Remember to regularly check for updates and new resources in the field of business credit. Continual learning and staying informed will help you make informed financial decisions for your business.

Thank you for reading this ebook, and we wish you continued success in your journey to build and manage your business credit profile!
This eBook aims to provide a comprehensive guide to building and managing business credit, offering

practical tips, strategies, and resources for entrepreneurs looking to establish a strong credit profile for their businesses.
Remember to stay updated with the latest regulations and practices in business credit as the landscape may evolve over time.